Java Design Patterns

A Guide to the 10 Most Effective Patterns of Software Development

Tejas M R

Copyright © 2023 Tejas M R

First release, March 2023

Contents

1 Introduction 7

1.1 **Overview of Design Patterns** — 7
1.2 **Why Java for Design Patterns?** — 7
1.2.1 Benefits of learning design patterns in Java: — 7
1.2.2 Drawbacks of learning design patterns in Java: — 8
1.3 **How are design patterns categorised?** — 8

2 Model-View-Controller Design Pattern 9

2.1 **Explanation of MVC design pattern for a high school student** — 9
2.2 **Explanation of MVC design pattern for a developer** — 9
2.3 **How to implement MVC design pattern in Java?** — 10
2.3.1 Model — 10
2.3.2 View — 11
2.3.3 Controller — 11
2.3.4 How to use the Model, View and Controller? — 12
2.4 **In what situations to use MVC design pattern?** — 12

3 Singleton Design Pattern 13

3.1 **Explanation of Singleton design pattern for a high school student** — 13
3.2 **Explanation of Singleton design pattern for a developer** — 13
3.3 **How to implement Singleton design pattern in Java?** — 14
3.4 **In what situations to use Singleton design pattern?** — 15

4 Factory Design Pattern ... 17
4.1 Explanation of Factory design pattern for a high school student — 17
4.2 Explanation of Factory design pattern for a developer — 17
4.3 How to implement Factory design pattern in Java? — 18
4.4 In what situations to use Factory design pattern? — 19

5 Observer Design Pattern ... 21
5.1 Explanation of Observer design pattern for a high school student — 21
5.2 Explanation of Observer design pattern for a developer — 21
5.3 How to implement Observer design pattern in Java? — 22
5.3.1 Create an interface for the observer objects: — 22
5.3.2 Create an interface for the subject: — 22
5.3.3 Create a concrete implementation of the subject: — 22
5.3.4 Create concrete implementations of the observer: — 23
5.3.5 Use the subject and observers in your application: — 23
5.3.6 Explanation — 23
5.4 In what situations to use Observer design pattern? — 23

6 Command Design Pattern ... 25
6.1 Explanation of Command design pattern for a high school student — 25
6.2 Explanation of Command design pattern for a developer — 25
6.3 How to implement Command design pattern in Java? — 26
6.3.1 Create the Command interface: — 26
6.3.2 Create concrete command classes that implement the Command interface: — 26
6.3.3 Create the Receiver class: — 26
6.3.4 Create the Invoker class: — 27
6.3.5 Use the Command pattern: — 27
6.3.6 Explanation — 27
6.4 In what situations to use Command design pattern? — 27

7 Adapter Design Pattern ... 29
7.1 Explanation of Adapter design pattern for a high school student — 29
7.2 Explanation of Adapter design pattern for a developer — 29
7.3 How to implement Adapter design pattern in Java? — 30
7.3.1 Create the target interface: — 30
7.3.2 Create the Adaptee class: — 30
7.3.3 Create the Adapter class: — 30
7.3.4 Client usage: — 30
7.4 In what situations to use Adapter design pattern? — 31

8 Decorator Design Pattern

8.1 Explanation of Decorator design pattern for a high school student
8.2 Explanation of Decorator design pattern for a developer
8.3 How to implement Decorator design pattern in Java?
8.3.1 Create an interface for the objects that will be decorated:
8.3.2 Create a concrete class that implements the Component interface:
8.3.3 Create an abstract class that implements the Component interface and acts as a base for the decorators:
8.3.4 Create concrete decorator classes that add additional behaviors to the decorated component:
8.3.5 Usage and Output
8.3.6 Explanation
8.4 In what situations to use Decorator design pattern?

9 Facade Design Pattern

9.1 Explanation of Facade design pattern for a high school student
9.2 Explanation of Facade design pattern for a developer
9.3 How to implement Facade design pattern in Java?
9.4 In what situations to use Facade design pattern?

10 Template Method Design Pattern

10.1 Explanation of Template Method design pattern for a high school student
10.2 Explanation of Template Method design pattern for a developer
10.3 How to implement Template Method design pattern in Java?
10.4 In what situations to use Template Method design pattern?

11 Composite Design Pattern

11.1 Explanation of Composite design pattern for a high school student
11.2 Explanation of Composite design pattern for a developer
11.3 How to implement Composite design pattern in Java?
11.4 In what situations to use Composite design pattern?

12 Conclusion

12.1 Recap of Design Patterns
12.2 Future of Design Patterns in Java
12.3 Recommended Further Reading and other resources

1. Introduction

1.1 Overview of Design Patterns

> **Definition 1.1.1 — Design Pattern.** Design patterns are reusable solutions to common problems that arise in software development.

Design patterns are an essential tool for software development that can help programmers write more organized, efficient, and reusable code. They are like pre-made templates for solving common problems that arise in software development, offering a standardized and proven solution for each problem. By using design patterns, programmers can save time, reduce the risk of bugs, and improve the overall quality of their code.

Design patterns are not specific to any particular programming language, but can be applied to a variety of languages, including Java. They are usually divided into categories such as creational, structural, and behavioral patterns, each with its own unique set of solutions.

For an average programmer, understanding design patterns is a crucial step in becoming a more experienced and efficient developer. Whether you're a beginner or an experienced programmer, incorporating design patterns into your work can help you create better, more maintainable code, and increase your value as a developer.

1.2 Why Java for Design Patterns?

1.2.1 Benefits of learning design patterns in Java:

- **Java is a widely used programming language:** As one of the most popular programming languages in the world, Java has a large user community and a wealth of resources, including books, online tutorials, and forums. By learning design patterns in Java, developers can benefit from this rich resource base and easily apply their knowledge to real-world projects.
- **Java supports object-oriented programming:** Java is an object-oriented language, and design patterns are primarily used in object-oriented programming. By learning design patterns in Java, developers can deepen their understanding of object-oriented concepts and improve their ability to design and implement complex software systems.
- **Java has a large library of pre-built classes:** Java has a large library of pre-built classes, including the Java Standard Library, which can be leveraged to implement design patterns more efficiently.

1.2.2 Drawbacks of learning design patterns in Java:

- **Design patterns can be language-agnostic:** Design patterns can be applied to any programming language, so focusing on one specific language, like Java, may limit the understanding of design patterns and their potential applications.
- **Java may not be the most efficient language for certain design patterns:** Depending on the specific design pattern, some other programming languages may offer more efficient solutions. For example, some functional programming languages may provide a more natural fit for certain design patterns, such as the Singleton pattern.

Despite these drawbacks, learning design patterns in Java is still a valuable skill for many developers. It provides a solid foundation for designing and implementing complex software systems, and the knowledge can be easily transferred to other programming languages.

1.3 How are design patterns categorised?

Design patterns are generally categorized into three main types:

1. **Creational Patterns:** These patterns are used to create objects and classes in a way that is suitable for a particular situation. Examples of creational patterns include the Factory Method, Abstract Factory, Singleton, and Builder patterns.
2. **Structural Patterns:** These patterns are used to arrange classes and objects to form larger structures. Examples of structural patterns include the Adapter, Bridge, Composite, and Decorator patterns.
3. **Behavioral Patterns:** These patterns are used to describe the ways in which objects interact and communicate with each other. Examples of behavioral patterns include the Observer, Chain of Responsibility, Command, and State patterns.

These categorizations are a useful way to understand the different types of design patterns and their intended uses. However, it is important to note that patterns can often overlap in terms of their functionality and that the exact categorization of a pattern may depend on the interpretation of the individual using it.

2. Model-View-Controller Design Pattern

> **Definition 2.0.1 — Model-View-Controller (MVC) Design Pattern.** MVC is a design pattern that separates the application logic into three parts: the model, the view, and the controller. The model represents the data, the view is responsible for presenting the data, and the controller handles the user's interaction with the data. This pattern helps in separating the concerns of an application and makes it easier to maintain and develop.

2.1 Explanation of MVC design pattern for a high school student

The Model-View-Controller (MVC) design pattern is a way of organizing code in software development that helps separate the data (model), the user interface (view), and the control logic (controller).

Think of a calculator. The buttons you press and the numbers that are displayed on the screen are the view. The underlying mathematical calculations performed by the calculator are the model. And the logic that connects the buttons you press to the calculations performed is the controller.

In software development, the MVC pattern helps keep the code organized, making it easier to maintain and update. For example, if you want to change the look of the calculator, you can do so without affecting the underlying calculations. Similarly, if you want to change the mathematical calculations performed, you can do so without affecting the user interface.

MVC is widely used in web development, where the model might represent data stored in a database, the view is the HTML and CSS that displays the data, and the controller is the code that handles user interactions, such as clicking a button or submitting a form.

So in summary, the MVC design pattern helps separate the different parts of a software application, making it easier to maintain and update.

2.2 Explanation of MVC design pattern for a developer

The Model-View-Controller (MVC) is a design pattern used to separate the application logic into three interconnected components: Model, View, and Controller.
   1. **Model:** Represents the data and business logic of the application. It is responsible for maintaining the state of the application and for providing methods to access the data.

2. **View:** Displays the data and user interface of the application. It is responsible for rendering the model data and for receiving user input.
3. **Controller:** Acts as an intermediary between the Model and View components. It is responsible for receiving user input, updating the Model, and for triggering updates to the View.

The separation of the components provides a number of benefits, including increased modularity, improved separation of concerns, and increased ease of testing and maintenance. It also enables the Model, View, and Controller components to be developed and tested independently, improving overall development efficiency.

In web development, the Model might represent a database or a web service, the View is the HTML, CSS and JavaScript code that is rendered in the user's browser, and the Controller is the server-side code that handles HTTP requests and updates the Model accordingly.

MVC is widely used in web development and has been adapted to many programming languages, including Java, Ruby on Rails, and ASP.NET. It remains a popular design pattern due to its simplicity, flexibility, and scalability.

2.3 How to implement MVC design pattern in Java?

Here is a high-level overview of how you can implement the Model-View-Controller (MVC) design pattern in Java:

2.3.1 Model

The model is responsible for storing and managing the data of the application. It should be an abstract class or interface, with the concrete implementations being POJOs (Plain Old Java Objects) that store the data.

Here's an example of a simple model for a user:

```java
public class User {
    private String firstName;
    private String lastName;

    public User(String firstName, String lastName) {
        this.firstName = firstName;
        this.lastName = lastName;
    }

    public String getFirstName() {
        return firstName;
    }

    public void setFirstName(String firstName) {
        this.firstName = firstName;
    }

    public String getLastName() {
        return lastName;
    }

    public void setLastName(String lastName) {
        this.lastName = lastName;
    }
}
```

2.3.2 View

The view is responsible for displaying the data to the user. It should be a separate class that takes a model object as input and uses its data to create the user interface.

Here's an example of a simple view for the user model:

```java
public class UserView {
    public void printUserDetails(User user) {
        System.out.println("User Details:");
        System.out.println("First Name: " + user.getFirstName());
        System.out.println("Last Name: " + user.getLastName());
    }
}
```

2.3.3 Controller

The controller is responsible for receiving user input and updating the model. It should be a separate class that takes a model object and a view object as inputs.

Here's an example of a simple controller for the user model:

```java
public class UserController {
    private User model;
    private UserView view;

    public UserController(User model, UserView view) {
        this.model = model;
        this.view = view;
    }

    public String getFirstName() {
        return model.getFirstName();
    }

    public void setFirstName(String firstName) {
        model.setFirstName(firstName);
    }

    public String getLastName() {
        return model.getLastName();
    }

    public void setLastName(String lastName) {
        model.setLastName(lastName);
    }

    public void updateView() {
        view.printUserDetails(model);
    }
}
```

2.3.4 How to use the Model, View and Controller?

Here's an example of how you can use the Model, View, and Controller to create an application:

```java
public class MVCExample {
    public static void main(String[] args) {
        User model = retrieveUserFromDatabase();

        UserView view = new UserView();

        UserController controller = new UserController(model, view);

        controller.updateView();

        controller.setFirstName("John");
        controller.setLastName("Doe");
        controller.updateView();
    }

    private static User retrieveUserFromDatabase() {
        User user = new User("Jane", "Doe");
        return user;
    }
}
```

2.4 In what situations to use MVC design pattern?

The Model-View-Controller (MVC) design pattern is typically used in situations where it is necessary to separate the concerns of data representation and user interaction. Some common scenarios where MVC may be used include:

- **Web Applications:** MVC is commonly used in web development to separate the presentation layer (View), the business logic (Model), and the user interaction (Controller).
- **Desktop Applications:** MVC can also be used in desktop applications where the user interface and the underlying data are separated for better organization and maintenance.
- **Large Applications:** MVC is especially useful in large applications, as it makes it easier to maintain and manage the codebase. By separating the concerns, changes to one component can be made without affecting the others, reducing the risk of introducing bugs.
- **Complex Business Logic:** MVC can also be used in situations where there is complex business logic that needs to be separated from the user interface. By using MVC, the logic can be encapsulated in the Model, making it easier to test and maintain.

Overall, MVC is a useful design pattern for creating applications that are scalable, maintainable, and have a clear separation of concerns.

3. Singleton Design Pattern

> **Definition 3.0.1 — Singleton Design Pattern.** Singleton is a design pattern that restricts a class to have only one instance, with a global point of access to it. This pattern is used when it is necessary to limit the number of instances of a class that can exist in the system, to ensure that there is only one instance of a class that controls the state of the application.

3.1 Explanation of Singleton design pattern for a high school student

The Singleton design pattern is a way to ensure that a class has only one instance at any given time. This can be useful in situations where you want to ensure that only one instance of an object exists in the system, such as when you have a class that represents a single resource that is shared across the application.

Imagine you are building a school library system. You want to keep track of all the books in the library, so you create a class called "Library." The Library class needs to be unique, so that no matter where you use it in the code, you always have access to the same instance of the class. This is where the Singleton pattern comes in.

With the Singleton pattern, you define a private constructor in the Library class, which ensures that no one can create a new instance of the class from outside. You also define a public method called "getInstance" that returns the single instance of the class. The first time the method is called, it creates a new instance of the Library class. Any subsequent calls to the method return the same instance that was created the first time.

In this way, you ensure that there is only one instance of the Library class in the entire system, and that all parts of the code can access the same data.

3.2 Explanation of Singleton design pattern for a developer

The Singleton design pattern is a creational pattern that ensures a class has only one instance while providing a single point of access to it for the entire application. This can be useful in situations where you want to maintain a single instance of a class to represent a shared resource, such as a database connection or a configuration manager.

The Singleton pattern is achieved by making the constructor of the class private, so that it cannot be instantiated directly. Instead, a public static method, often referred to as the "getInstance" method, is provided that returns the single instance of the class. The first time the method is called, it creates a new instance of the class, and all subsequent calls return the same instance.

The Singleton pattern can be implemented in various ways, but it is essential to ensure that only one instance of the class is created, and that it is accessible from anywhere in the code. To achieve this, it is common to use lazy initialization, where the instance is created only when it is first needed.

In summary, the Singleton pattern can be useful for creating shared resources in a system where it is important to maintain a single instance and ensure that it is accessible from anywhere in the code. It can also be used to control the instantiation of a class, ensuring that it is only created once, and to provide a single point of access to the instance.

3.3 How to implement Singleton design pattern in Java?

Here is an example of how to implement the Singleton design pattern in Java:

```java
public class Singleton {
    private static Singleton instance = null;
    private Singleton() {}

    public static Singleton getInstance() {
        if (instance == null) {
            instance = new Singleton();
        }
        return instance;
    }
}
```

In this example, the Singleton class has a private constructor that ensures that it cannot be instantiated directly. Instead, a public static method called getInstance is provided, which returns the single instance of the class.

The first time the getInstance method is called, it creates a new instance of the Singleton class by calling the private constructor. Subsequent calls to getInstance return the same instance that was created the first time.

It's worth noting that this implementation is not thread-safe, so if multiple threads attempt to access the getInstance method simultaneously, it is possible for multiple instances of the Singleton class to be created. To ensure thread safety, you can use synchronization, for example:

```java
public class Singleton {
    private static Singleton instance = null;
    private Singleton() {}

    public static synchronized Singleton getInstance() {
        if (instance == null) {
            instance = new Singleton();
        }
        return instance;
    }
}
```

In this example, the getInstance method is declared as synchronized, ensuring that only one thread can access it at a time. This ensures that the Singleton pattern is correctly implemented, even in a multi-threaded environment.

3.4 In what situations to use Singleton design pattern?

The Singleton design pattern is used in the following situations:

- When you want to ensure that a class has only one instance throughout the entire application, and you want to provide a single point of access to it. For example, a logging service, database connection, or configuration manager.
- When you want to ensure that a class is instantiated only once and its instance is accessible from anywhere in the code. This can be useful for implementing shared resources in a system.
- When you want to restrict the instantiation of a class to only one instance and ensure that it is only created when it is first needed. This can be useful for reducing memory usage and improving performance in some cases.
- When you want to control the instantiation of a class, ensuring that it is only created once, and that it is accessible from anywhere in the code.

It is important to use the Singleton design pattern judiciously and only when it is necessary. Overuse of the Singleton pattern can lead to tightly coupled code and make it more difficult to maintain and test your application.

4. Factory Design Pattern

> **Definition 4.0.1 — Factory Design Pattern.** Factory is a design pattern that provides an interface for creating objects in a superclass, but allows subclasses to alter the type of objects that will be created. This pattern is used to create objects without specifying the exact class of object that will be created.

4.1 Explanation of Factory design pattern for a high school student

The Factory design pattern is a way of creating objects in an object-oriented programming language. Imagine you have a car factory. The factory makes cars. When you order a car, you specify the type of car you want (e.g. sedan, SUV, sports car, etc.). The factory then builds the car for you and delivers it to you.

Similarly, in the Factory design pattern, you have a factory class that creates objects of different types. When you ask the factory to create an object, you specify the type of object you want. The factory then creates the object for you and returns it to you. This allows you to separate the process of creating objects from the rest of your code, making it easier to change the way objects are created if needed.

Think of the factory as a kind of "object-making machine." Instead of writing code to create objects, you tell the factory what you want, and it creates the objects for you. This makes your code easier to read and maintain, and makes it easier to change how objects are created if needed.

4.2 Explanation of Factory design pattern for a developer

The Factory design pattern is a creational pattern that provides an interface for creating objects in a superclass, but allows subclasses to alter the type of objects that will be created. The Factory design pattern is often used in situations where a class cannot anticipate the type of objects it needs to create.

For example, consider a class that needs to create objects to represent different shapes (e.g. rectangle, triangle, circle, etc.). Instead of using a constructor to create these objects, the class can use a factory method that takes the necessary parameters to create the object and returns the object to the caller.

The Factory design pattern provides several benefits:

- Abstraction: It separates the implementation details of object creation from the client code, allowing the client code to focus on the task at hand and not the details of object creation.
- Flexibility: The Factory design pattern allows you to add new types of objects to your application without having to modify the client code. This makes it easier to maintain and extend your application.

- Reusability: By encapsulating the details of object creation in a factory class, you can reuse the factory in multiple parts of your application, making your code more modular and easier to maintain.

Overall, the Factory design pattern provides a clean and flexible way to create objects in an object-oriented programming language. It allows you to encapsulate the details of object creation, making your code more maintainable and reusable.

4.3 How to implement Factory design pattern in Java?

Here's an example of how to implement the Factory design pattern in Java:

```java
interface Shape {
   void draw();
}

class Rectangle implements Shape {
   @Override public void draw() {
      System.out.println("Inside Rectangle::draw() method.");
   }
}

class Square implements Shape {
   @Override public void draw() {
      System.out.println("Inside Square::draw() method.");
   }
}

class Circle implements Shape {
   @Override public void draw() {
      System.out.println("Inside Circle::draw() method.");
   }
}

class ShapeFactory {
   //use getShape method to get object of type shape
   public Shape getShape(String shapeType){
      if(shapeType == null){
         return null;
      }
      if(shapeType.equalsIgnoreCase("CIRCLE")){
         return new Circle();
      } else if(shapeType.equalsIgnoreCase("RECTANGLE")){
         return new Rectangle();
      } else if(shapeType.equalsIgnoreCase("SQUARE")){
         return new Square();
      }
      return null;
   }
}

public class FactoryPatternDemo {
   public static void main(String[] args) {
      ShapeFactory shapeFactory = new ShapeFactory();
      //get an object of Circle and call its draw method.
```

```
            Shape shape1 = shapeFactory.getShape("CIRCLE");
            //call draw method of Circle
            shape1.draw();
            //get an object of Rectangle and call its draw method.
            Shape shape2 = shapeFactory.getShape("RECTANGLE");
            //call draw method of Rectangle
            shape2.draw();
            //get an object of Square and call its draw method.
            Shape shape3 = shapeFactory.getShape("SQUARE");
            //call draw method of square
            shape3.draw();
    }
}
```

In this example, we have an interface Shape and three classes that implement the Shape interface: Rectangle, Square, and Circle. The ShapeFactory class is the factory class that creates objects of the Shape interface. The getShape method of the ShapeFactory class takes a String argument and returns an object of the appropriate Shape implementation.

In the main method, we create an instance of the ShapeFactory class and use it to create objects of the Shape interface by calling the getShape method and passing the appropriate String argument. This allows us to create objects of the Shape interface without having to worry about the implementation details, making our code more flexible and maintainable.

4.4 In what situations to use Factory design pattern?

The Factory Design Pattern is used in situations where you need to create objects of similar types, but the type of objects to be created can be decided at runtime. It is used when a class cannot anticipate the type of objects it needs to create. The Factory Method provides a way to delegate the instantiation logic to its subclasses.

Some common use cases of the Factory Pattern include:
- When a class cannot anticipate the type of objects it needs to create
- When a class wants its subclasses to specify the objects it creates
- When classes delegate responsibility to one of several helper subclasses, and you want to localize the knowledge of which helper subclass is the delegate.

Examples of situations where the Factory Pattern can be used include:
- when creating objects for UI elements, such as buttons or panels, based on user input or configuration data
- when implementing a plugin architecture where objects of different types can be created based on user-selected options
- when managing the creation of objects that are part of a larger system, such as creating database connections based on configuration data.

5. Observer Design Pattern

Definition 5.0.1 — Observer Design Pattern. Observer is a design pattern that defines a one-to-many dependency between objects, so that when one object changes state, all its dependents are notified and updated automatically. This pattern is used to implement dynamic systems, where the state of one object affects the state of others.

5.1 Explanation of Observer design pattern for a high school student

The Observer Design Pattern is a way for one object, known as the subject, to send updates to multiple other objects, known as observers, when it changes. Think of it like a teacher sending updates to students about their grades. The teacher is the subject and the students are the observers.

The subject keeps track of a list of its observers, and whenever it changes, it sends an update to all of them. This way, the observers stay in sync with the subject, and the subject can change without affecting the observers directly.

An example of this pattern in real life could be a weather service sending updates to different weather apps when the weather changes. The weather service is the subject and the weather apps are the observers.

This pattern can be useful in situations where multiple objects need to stay updated with the state of a single object, and the objects do not need to interact directly with each other.

5.2 Explanation of Observer design pattern for a developer

The Observer Design Pattern is a way for one object, known as the subject, to notify multiple other objects, known as observers, about changes in its state. The subject maintains a list of its observers and notifies them when its state changes.

This pattern can be useful in situations where multiple objects need to be notified about changes to a single object, and the objects should not interact directly with each other. This can help to decouple the objects and make the system more flexible and maintainable.

In terms of implementation, the subject and observer objects need to have a common interface, and the subject needs to maintain a list of observers and provide methods for adding and removing observers. The observer objects need to implement the interface and provide a method to receive notifications from the subject. When the subject changes, it calls the update method on each of its observers to notify them of the change.

This pattern is widely used in many different applications, such as GUI applications, event-driven systems, and reactive programming. It is a fundamental pattern that can help you to design more flexible and scalable systems.

5.3 How to implement Observer design pattern in Java?

Here's an example of how to implement the Observer Design Pattern in Java:

5.3.1 Create an interface for the observer objects:

```java
public interface Observer {
    void update(Subject subject);
}
```

5.3.2 Create an interface for the subject:

```java
public interface Subject {
    void registerObserver(Observer observer);
    void removeObserver(Observer observer);
    void notifyObservers();
}
```

5.3.3 Create a concrete implementation of the subject:

```java
public class ConcreteSubject implements Subject {
    private List<Observer> observers = new ArrayList<>();
    private int state;

    public int getState() {
        return state;
    }

    public void setState(int state) {
        this.state = state;
        notifyObservers();
    }

    @Override
    public void registerObserver(Observer observer) {
        observers.add(observer);
    }

    @Override
    public void removeObserver(Observer observer) {
        observers.remove(observer);
    }

    @Override
    public void notifyObservers() {
        for (Observer observer : observers) {
```

```java
            observer.update(this);
        }
    }
}
```

5.3.4 Create concrete implementations of the observer:

```java
public class ConcreteObserverA implements Observer {
    @Override
    public void update(Subject subject) {
        int state = subject.getState();
        // Update state of observer based on change in subject
    }
}

public class ConcreteObserverB implements Observer {
    @Override
    public void update(Subject subject) {
        int state = subject.getState();
        // Update state of observer based on change in subject
    }
}
```

5.3.5 Use the subject and observers in your application:

```java
public class Main {
    public static void main(String[] args) {
        ConcreteSubject subject = new ConcreteSubject();
        ConcreteObserverA observerA = new ConcreteObserverA();
        ConcreteObserverB observerB = new ConcreteObserverB();
        subject.registerObserver(observerA);
        subject.registerObserver(observerB);
        subject.setState(5);
    }
}
```

5.3.6 Explanation

This code implements the Observer Design Pattern in Java by defining an interface for the observer objects, an interface for the subject, concrete implementations of both the subject and observer, and using them in an application. When the state of the subject changes, it calls the notifyObservers method, which in turn calls the update method on each of its observers, allowing them to react to the change in the subject's state.

5.4 In what situations to use Observer design pattern?

The Observer design pattern is typically used in situations where there is a one-to-many relationship between objects and when changes in one object need to be reflected in other objects. Some common use cases of the Observer pattern are:

1. Implementing a model-view-controller architecture where changes in the model are notified to the views.
2. Implementing event-driven systems, such as user interfaces, where changes in one component trigger updates in other components.
3. Implementing a publish-subscribe system where events are published to multiple subscribers.
4. Implementing a logging system, where changes in the log data need to be notified to multiple log listeners.
5. Implementing a stock ticker system, where changes in the stock prices need to be notified to multiple subscribers.

In all these use cases, the Observer pattern allows the objects to be loosely coupled, so that changes in one object don't affect the other objects directly. Instead, the changes are notified to the objects that need to be updated.

6. Command Design Pattern

> **Definition 6.0.1 — Command Design Pattern.** Command is a design pattern that encapsulates a request as an object, thereby allowing for the parameterization of clients with different requests, queuing or logging of requests, and support for undoable operations.

6.1 Explanation of Command design pattern for a high school student

The Command design pattern is a way to encapsulate actions into objects. Imagine you want to turn off a light, you could walk to the switch and turn it off yourself, or you could ask someone else to do it for you. In this case, you are the client and the person you ask is the receiver. But instead of asking a person, you could give a command, such as "Turn off the light", to an object, the command object. The command object then asks the receiver, the light, to turn off.

Think of the Command design pattern like giving someone a to-do list. The to-do list contains a list of tasks that need to be done, and the person follows the list to complete each task. In this case, the to-do list is the command object and the person is the receiver.

In software development, the Command design pattern can be used to implement undo/redo functionality, where the command objects represent the actions that can be undone or redone. It can also be used to implement deferred execution of operations, where the operations are represented as command objects that are executed at a later time.

6.2 Explanation of Command design pattern for a developer

The Command design pattern is a behavioral design pattern that encapsulates a request as an object, thereby letting you parameterize clients with different requests, queue or log requests, and support undo-redo operations.

In this pattern, a command object is created for each request, and the command object is executed by an invoker. The command object knows which receiver to call and what to call on the receiver. The invoker decides when to execute the command, and the client decides what commands to execute.

The Command pattern decouples the sender of a request from its receiver, allowing the receiver to be changed without affecting the sender. It also provides a way to queue requests and execute them later.

This pattern is commonly used in GUI applications, where a user triggers a command, such as "Save", "Open", "Print", etc. The commands can be executed immediately or queued for execution at a later time. The pattern is also used in game development, where commands are used to represent game actions, such as "Move", "Shoot", "Jump", etc.

The Command pattern can be implemented in Java using interfaces, abstract classes, and concrete classes. The invoker, the command, and the receiver are the key components in the Command pattern. The invoker holds a command object, the command holds a reference to the receiver, and the receiver performs the action when the execute() method of the command is called.

6.3 How to implement Command design pattern in Java?

Here is a basic example of how to implement the Command design pattern in Java:

6.3.1 Create the Command interface:

```java
public interface Command {
  void execute();
}
```

6.3.2 Create concrete command classes that implement the Command interface:

```java
public class LightOnCommand implements Command {
  private Light light;

  public LightOnCommand(Light light) {
    this.light = light;
  }

  @Override
  public void execute() {
    light.on();
  }
}

public class LightOffCommand implements Command {
  private Light light;

  public LightOffCommand(Light light) {
    this.light = light;
  }

  @Override
  public void execute() {
    light.off();
  }
}
```

6.3.3 Create the Receiver class:

```java
public class Light {
```

```java
    public void on() {
        System.out.println("Light is on");
    }

    public void off() {
        System.out.println("Light is off");
    }
}
```

6.3.4 Create the Invoker class:

```java
public class Switch {
    private List<Command> commands = new ArrayList<>();

    public void storeAndExecute(Command command) {
        commands.add(command);
        command.execute();
    }
}
```

6.3.5 Use the Command pattern:

```java
public class Main {
    public static void main(String[] args) {
        Light light = new Light();
        Command lightOnCommand = new LightOnCommand(light);
        Command lightOffCommand = new LightOffCommand(light);
        Switch switch = new Switch();

        switch.storeAndExecute(lightOnCommand);
        switch.storeAndExecute(lightOffCommand);
    }
}
```

6.3.6 Explanation

This code creates a Light class as the receiver, LightOnCommand and LightOffCommand as concrete command classes, and Switch as the invoker. When the storeAndExecute() method of the Switch class is called, the specified command is executed, which results in the on() or off() method of the Light class being called.

6.4 In what situations to use Command design pattern?

The Command design pattern is used in situations where you want to decouple the object that invokes an operation (invoker) from the object that performs the operation (receiver). This can be useful when you want to:

1. Queue or log requests: you can store a list of commands in a queue and execute them one by one.
2. Implement undo/redo: you can store a list of commands in a stack and revert the execution by popping the stack.

3. Parameterize objects with operations: you can pass commands as parameters to objects and execute them dynamically.
4. Implement deferred execution of operations: you can execute operations later, after the invoker has finished its work.

In Java, you can implement the Command design pattern by creating a common interface for all commands, which declares a single execute() method. Concrete command classes implement this method by calling a specific operation on the receiver object. The invoker object has a reference to the command, and it executes it by calling the execute() method.

7. Adapter Design Pattern

> **Definition 7.0.1 — Adapter Design Pattern.** Adapter is a design pattern that converts the interface of a class into another interface that the clients expect. This pattern is used when two existing classes have incompatible interfaces and we want to provide a bridge between them.

7.1 Explanation of Adapter design pattern for a high school student

The Adapter design pattern is a way to make two things work together that were not designed to work together originally. Imagine you have a toy that you want to plug into a wall socket to make it work, but the toy has a different type of plug than the wall socket. To make it work, you need an adapter that changes the toy's plug into the type of plug that fits into the wall socket.

In a similar way, the Adapter design pattern allows two incompatible classes to work together by converting the interface of one class into another that the client is expecting. This way, you can reuse existing classes in your code, even if they do not match the interface that you need.

For a high school student, you can think of the Adapter design pattern as a way to make things work together that were not meant to work together from the beginning.

7.2 Explanation of Adapter design pattern for a developer

The Adapter design pattern is a structural pattern that allows two incompatible interfaces to work together. It is often used when a class wants to use another class, but the interfaces are not compatible. The Adapter pattern allows the class to use the other class by converting its interface into a form that the first class can work with.

The key idea behind the Adapter pattern is to change the way objects interact with each other. An adapter acts as a bridge between two classes, converting the interface of one class into another that the client is expecting. This way, the client can use the adapted class without having to modify its code, and the adapted class can be used in a wider range of situations.

In software development, the Adapter design pattern is often used to integrate legacy systems or third-party libraries into new applications. It can also be used to make existing code more flexible and reusable by allowing it to work with new classes that it was not designed to work with originally.

7.3 How to implement Adapter design pattern in Java?

Here's an example of how to implement the Adapter design pattern in Java:

7.3.1 Create the target interface:

This is the interface that the client class is expecting.

```java
public interface Target {
   void request();
}
```

7.3.2 Create the Adaptee class:

This is the class that we want to adapt. It has a different interface than the target.

```java
public class Adaptee {
   public void specificRequest() {
      System.out.println("Specific request.");
   }
}
```

7.3.3 Create the Adapter class:

This class implements the target interface and adapts the Adaptee class to the target interface.

```java
public class Adapter implements Target {
   private Adaptee adaptee;

   public Adapter(Adaptee adaptee) {
      this.adaptee = adaptee;
   }

   @Override
   public void request() {
      adaptee.specificRequest();
   }
}
```

7.3.4 Client usage:

The client can use the Adapter class by creating an instance of it and calling its request() method.

```java
public class Client {
   public static void main(String[] args) {
      Adaptee adaptee = new Adaptee();
      Target target = new Adapter(adaptee);
      target.request();
   }
}
```

This example demonstrates how to implement the Adapter design pattern in Java, but you can apply this pattern to various situations, and modify it to fit your specific needs.

7.4 In what situations to use Adapter design pattern?

The adapter design pattern is used when you want to use an existing class, but its interface is incompatible with the rest of the code. The adapter pattern allows you to create a new adapter class that wraps the existing class, translating its methods into a form that the client code can understand. The adapter design pattern is commonly used in software development when new systems are being integrated with older systems or when different components need to work together. The goal of using an adapter is to allow these incompatible classes to work together by providing a common interface between them.

8. Decorator Design Pattern

> **Definition 8.0.1 — Decorator Design Pattern.** Decorator is a design pattern that allows the behavior of a class to be altered dynamically by adding new behavior to it without changing its source code. This pattern is used when we want to add new behavior to objects, without affecting the behavior of other objects from the same class.

8.1 Explanation of Decorator design pattern for a high school student

The decorator design pattern is a design pattern that allows you to add new functionality to an existing object, without changing its structure. This is achieved by wrapping the original object in a decorator object. The decorator object has the same interface as the original object, so it can be used in the same way as the original object, but it also adds new behavior to the object.

Think of it like adding decorations to a Christmas tree. The tree is the original object and the decorations are the new functionality that you want to add. The decorations don't change the structure of the tree, they just add to it.

This pattern is useful in situations where you want to add new behavior to an existing object, but don't want to change its structure. It's also useful when you want to add different types of functionality to an object, depending on the situation.

8.2 Explanation of Decorator design pattern for a developer

The decorator design pattern is a structural pattern that allows adding new behaviors to an existing object dynamically, by wrapping the object in one or more decorator objects. The decorator objects have the same interface as the original object, so they can be used interchangeably in the application code.

This pattern is useful in situations where you need to add new functionality to an object, but don't want to make changes to the object's source code. It provides a flexible alternative to subclassing, which can lead to an explosion of classes in case you need to add multiple functionalities to the same object.

The decorator pattern is commonly used in Java to implement dynamic proxies, where you need to add additional behavior to an object, such as logging, transaction management, or security checks, without modifying the original object. It's also used in GUI programming to add new functionalities to UI components, such as adding a border, a scrollbar, or a shadow to a text area.

8.3 How to implement Decorator design pattern in Java?

Here is an example of how to implement the decorator design pattern in Java:

8.3.1 Create an interface for the objects that will be decorated:

```java
public interface Component {
    void operation();
}
```

8.3.2 Create a concrete class that implements the Component interface:

```java
public class ConcreteComponent implements Component {
    public void operation() {
        System.out.println("Concrete Component Operation");
    }
}
```

8.3.3 Create an abstract class that implements the Component interface and acts as a base for the decorators:

```java
public abstract class Decorator implements Component {
    protected Component component;

    public Decorator(Component component) {
        this.component = component;
    }

    public void operation() {
        component.operation();
    }
}
```

8.3.4 Create concrete decorator classes that add additional behaviors to the decorated component:

```java
public class ConcreteDecoratorA extends Decorator {
    public ConcreteDecoratorA(Component component) {
        super(component);
    }

    @Override
    public void operation() {
        super.operation();
        System.out.println("Concrete Decorator A Operation");
    }
}

public class ConcreteDecoratorB extends Decorator {
    public ConcreteDecoratorB(Component component) {
```

```
    super(component);
  }

  @Override
  public void operation() {
    super.operation();
    System.out.println("Concrete Decorator B Operation");
  }
}
```

8.3.5 Usage and Output

To use the decorator pattern, you can create a ConcreteComponent object and wrap it in one or more ConcreteDecorator objects:

```
public class Client {
  public static void main(String[] args) {
    Component component = new ConcreteComponent();
    component = new ConcreteDecoratorA(component);
    component = new ConcreteDecoratorB(component);
    component.operation();
  }
}
```

This code will produce the following output:

```
Concrete Component Operation
Concrete Decorator A Operation
Concrete Decorator B Operation
```

8.3.6 Explanation

As you can see, the decorator pattern allows you to add new functionalities to an object dynamically, by wrapping the object in one or more decorator objects. The decorator objects have the same interface as the original object, so they can be used interchangeably in the application code.

8.4 In what situations to use Decorator design pattern?

The Decorator design pattern is used when you want to add or extend the functionality of an existing object dynamically, without changing the object's structure. This pattern is commonly used in situations where you have objects with multiple responsibilities, and you want to add responsibilities to specific objects dynamically. For example, in a graphics editor application, you might have a shape object, and you want to add border or fill color to the shape. With the Decorator pattern, you can add the desired functionality without changing the existing object's code, but by creating new objects that wrap around the original object.

9. Facade Design Pattern

> **Definition 9.0.1 — Facade Design Pattern.** Facade is a design pattern that provides a simplified interface to a complex system of classes. This pattern is used to provide a unified and simpler interface to a set of interfaces in a subsystem, thereby hiding the complexity of the subsystem from the client.

9.1 Explanation of Facade design pattern for a high school student

The Facade design pattern is a way to simplify complex systems by providing a single, unified interface to multiple, smaller, underlying systems. Imagine you want to play a video game, but there are many different parts of the game that need to work together to make it run properly. The Facade pattern is like having a single button you can press that takes care of all the different parts, making it easier for you to play the game. In software, a Facade is a class that provides a simplified interface to a complex system, hiding the underlying complexity and making it easier to use. This pattern can be useful in situations where you want to simplify the interface to a complex system, or when you want to provide a unified, high-level interface to a set of smaller, related components.

9.2 Explanation of Facade design pattern for a developer

The Facade Design Pattern is a structural design pattern that provides a simplified interface to a complex system. It acts as an interface between the client and a complex system, hiding the underlying complexity and providing a simpler, more unified, and easy-to-use interface.

For example, consider a system with multiple classes and objects with complex functionalities and interactions. Rather than having the client directly interact with all these classes and objects, the Facade Design Pattern can be applied to create a single, unified interface that the client can interact with. This interface can simplify the interaction with the complex system, making it easier to understand, use, and maintain.

In Java, the Facade Design Pattern can be implemented by creating a class that implements the simplified interface, and delegates calls to the classes and objects that make up the complex system. The implementation details and code will vary depending on the specific requirements and complexities of the system being simplified.

9.3 How to implement Facade design pattern in Java?

The facade design pattern provides a simplified interface to a complex subsystem. The idea is to hide the complexities of the system and provide a unified and simple API for the client to access the system. The facade pattern involves a single class which provides simplified methods required by the client and delegates calls to methods of existing system classes.

Here is an example implementation in Java:

```java
public class ComputerFacade {
    private final CPU processor;
    private final Memory ram;
    private final HardDrive hd;

    public ComputerFacade() {
        this.processor = new CPU();
        this.ram = new Memory();
        this.hd = new HardDrive();
    }

    public void start() {
        processor.freeze();
        ram.load(BOOT_ADDRESS, hd.read(BOOT_SECTOR, SECTOR_SIZE));
        processor.jump(BOOT_ADDRESS);
        processor.execute();
    }
}
```

In this example, the ComputerFacade class provides a simplified API for starting the computer. The client does not need to know about the details of the CPU, memory, and hard drive. The facade class delegates the start method calls to the methods of existing classes.

9.4 In what situations to use Facade design pattern?

The facade design pattern is used in situations where a complex system or subsystem needs to be simplified for easier use. It provides a unified interface to a set of interactions in a subsystem, hiding the complexity behind it. This can make the subsystem easier to use and can also reduce the coupling between the client code and the subsystem. It is often used in applications where there is a need to present a simplified view of an underlying system.

Examples of when to use the facade pattern include:

- When you want to provide a simple interface to a complex system
- When you want to reduce coupling between a client and a subsystem
- When you want to wrap a poorly designed collection of APIs with a single, well-designed API

The facade pattern can be implemented in Java by creating a class that acts as a simplified interface to the complex subsystem. This class delegates calls to the appropriate objects in the subsystem and can hide the complexity of the underlying system from the client code.

10. Template Method Design Pattern

> **Definition 10.0.1 — Template Method Design Pattern.** Template Method is a design pattern that defines the skeleton of an algorithm in a method, with subclasses providing specific implementation of steps. This pattern is used to allow a class to be defined with a standard way of performing a particular operation, with subclasses providing specific implementation of the steps involved in the operation.

10.1 Explanation of Template Method design pattern for a high school student

The template method design pattern is a way to create a standardized procedure for solving a problem. It provides a set of steps that must be followed in a specific order to solve the problem. Think of it like a recipe for cooking a dish. Just like a recipe, the template method pattern provides a basic outline, but it allows you to customize and add your own variations to the solution.

For a high school student, you can think of the template method pattern like creating a study plan. A study plan outlines the steps you need to take to study for a test, but you can adjust the plan to fit your own learning style and needs. This can make studying more efficient and effective.

10.2 Explanation of Template Method design pattern for a developer

The template method design pattern is a behavioral design pattern that defines the program skeleton of an algorithm in a method, called the template method, which provides a standard way of executing the algorithm. The subclasses of the algorithm can then override certain steps of the algorithm without changing its structure.

This pattern is useful when you have a common behavior among objects that can be modified in a limited way. The template method can provide a blueprint for the behavior and the concrete subclasses can implement the required modifications to that behavior. This leads to a cleaner and more maintainable codebase, since common behavior is encapsulated in a single place and variations are handled by subclasses.

The template method design pattern can be implemented in Java by defining a base class with a template method that implements the algorithm and providing hooks, or abstract methods, for the subclasses to override. The subclasses then provide their own implementation for the hooks, if necessary, to customize the behavior.

10.3 How to implement Template Method design pattern in Java?

The template method design pattern is a behavioral design pattern that provides a blueprint for implementing a certain algorithm, allowing subclasses to provide specific steps while preserving the overall structure. In Java, it can be implemented using abstract classes and method overriding.

Here's an example of how to implement the template method design pattern in Java:

```java
abstract class Game {
   abstract void initialize();
   abstract void startPlay();
   abstract void endPlay();

   //template method
   public final void play() {
      initialize();
      startPlay();
      endPlay();
   }
}

class Cricket extends Game {
   @Override
   void endPlay() {
      System.out.println("Cricket Game Finished!");
   }

   @Override
   void initialize() {
      System.out.println("Cricket Game Initialized! Start playing.");
   }

   @Override
   void startPlay() {
      System.out.println("Cricket Game Started. Enjoy the game!");
   }
}

class Football extends Game {
   @Override
   void endPlay() {
      System.out.println("Football Game Finished!");
   }

   @Override
   void initialize() {
      System.out.println("Football Game Initialized! Start playing.");
   }

   @Override
   void startPlay() {
      System.out.println("Football Game Started. Enjoy the game!");
   }
}
```

```
public class TemplatePatternDemo {
   public static void main(String[] args) {
      Game game = new Cricket();
      game.play();
      System.out.println();
      game = new Football();
      game.play();
   }
}
```

The template method pattern is useful in situations where you want to provide a default implementation for a certain algorithm, while allowing subclasses to provide their own specific implementation for certain steps.

10.4 In what situations to use Template Method design pattern?

The template method design pattern is used in situations where you want to define the skeleton of an algorithm, but allow subclasses to provide the implementation for some of the steps. The template method design pattern allows you to provide a common interface for a group of related algorithms, and it also allows you to change the algorithms independently from the clients that use them.

An example of when to use the template method design pattern is when you are implementing a common task that has multiple steps, and some of the steps may change based on specific requirements. By using the template method pattern, you can define the basic steps and let subclasses implement the specific details for each step. This way, you can maintain the common interface, but still provide the flexibility to change the algorithms as needed.

11. Composite Design Pattern

> **Definition 11.0.1 — Composite Design Pattern.** Composite is a design pattern that composes objects into a tree structure to represent a part-whole hierarchy. This pattern is used to represent a hierarchical structure, where some objects are composed of other objects, allowing clients to treat both individual objects and compositions of objects in a uniform way.

11.1 Explanation of Composite design pattern for a high school student

The composite design pattern is a way of building structures with objects that can be either a single item or a collection of items. It allows us to treat individual objects and groups of objects in the same way. This pattern is often used to build user interfaces or to manage tree-like data structures where we want to process a whole tree of objects as if they were a single entity.

Think of a tree where each leaf is a single object and each branch is a collection of leaves and branches. The composite design pattern lets us work with this tree structure as if it were a single object, even though it is made up of many individual objects.

A simple example could be a file system. A file is an individual object and a folder is a collection of files and other folders. The composite pattern allows us to treat a folder and a file in the same way, as an object that we can manipulate, even though a folder is made up of multiple objects.

11.2 Explanation of Composite design pattern for a developer

The Composite design pattern is a structural pattern that is used to represent a tree-like structure of objects, where each object can be either a leaf node or a composite node, which is made up of multiple leaf or composite nodes. This pattern allows you to represent a group of objects as a single object, making it easier to treat them as a unit. The Composite pattern is used in many applications to build complex structures, such as hierarchical data structures, menu systems, and document trees. The Composite pattern is usually implemented using the concept of recursive composition, where each node in the tree-like structure contains a reference to a collection of other nodes. This enables you to manipulate the entire tree structure in a consistent way, regardless of whether you're dealing with leaf nodes or composite nodes.

11.3 How to implement Composite design pattern in Java?

The composite design pattern is used to represent a tree-like structure of objects where each object can either be a composite object containing other objects or a leaf object that cannot contain any other objects. In Java, this pattern can be implemented by creating a Component interface that defines the operations to be performed on objects in the composite structure. This interface should include methods such as add() and remove() to manage the child components, and a method such as operation() that performs some action on the object.

The Leaf class implements the Component interface and represents the leaf objects in the tree structure. The Composite class extends the Component interface and represents the composite objects in the tree structure. It includes methods to add and remove child components and to perform some action on the object.

Here's an example implementation in Java:

```java
interface Component {
    void operation();
}

class Leaf implements Component {
    @Override
    public void operation() {
        // Implementation for the leaf object
    }
}

class Composite implements Component {
    private List<Component> components = new ArrayList<>();

    @Override
    public void operation() {
        // Implementation for the composite object
        for (Component component : components) {
            component.operation();
        }
    }

    public void add(Component component) {
        components.add(component);
    }

    public void remove(Component component) {
        components.remove(component);
    }
}
```

The composite design pattern is useful when you need to represent a complex structure of objects that can be composed of simpler objects and when you need to perform actions on the objects in the structure in a uniform manner, regardless of whether they are composite objects or leaf objects.

11.4 In what situations to use Composite design pattern?

The composite design pattern is used in situations where you need to represent a part-whole hierarchy of objects. This pattern allows you to treat individual objects and compositions of objects in the same way.

An example of this could be representing the hierarchical structure of a company, where each department is considered an object and a collection of departments makes up the whole company.

Another example could be representing a file system, where each file and folder can be treated as an object. Folders can contain files and other folders, making up a tree-like structure.

By using the composite pattern, you can manipulate the individual objects and compositions of objects in a uniform manner, without having to worry about the underlying implementation details. This can make your code more flexible and maintainable.

12. Conclusion

12.1 Recap of Design Patterns

Design patterns are a set of solutions to recurring software design problems that arise in the development of large-scale systems. They provide a way to organize code, increase maintainability, and reduce complexity. There are several categories of design patterns including creational, structural, and behavioral patterns. Each design pattern has a specific intent and a set of steps to implement it in a software design. Some commonly known design patterns include the Singleton, Factory, Observer, Command, Adapter, Decorator, Facade, Template Method, and Composite patterns. By understanding and applying design patterns, developers can improve the quality and efficiency of their code.

12.2 Future of Design Patterns in Java

The future of design patterns in Java looks bright as they are still widely used and recognized as best practices in software development. Java has evolved over the years to provide more efficient and powerful ways of implementing design patterns, but the basic principles behind them remain the same. As long as software development continues to progress and new technologies emerge, design patterns will continue to play an important role in helping developers solve common software problems in an organized and efficient manner. As long as there is a need for clear and maintainable code, design patterns will be a valuable tool for Java developers.

12.3 Recommended Further Reading and other resources

If you are interested in learning more about design patterns, there are several great resources available. Here are a few recommendations:

1. "Design Patterns: Elements of Reusable Object-Oriented Software" by Erich Gamma, Richard Helm, Ralph Johnson, and John Vlissides. This is the classic book on design patterns and is often considered the definitive guide to the subject.
2. "Head First Design Patterns" by Eric Freeman and Elisabeth Freeman. This is a more accessible, hands-on approach to learning design patterns and is a great choice for developers who prefer a more visual and interactive learning experience.

3. "Java Design Patterns: A Guide to Object-Oriented Design" by Markus Schoeler. This book focuses specifically on design patterns in Java and provides practical, code-based examples of each pattern.
4. "Design Patterns in Java" video course by Derek Banas. This video course provides a comprehensive introduction to design patterns in Java and includes a variety of examples and exercises to help you practice what you have learned.
5. The Gang of Four website (gof.com). This website is dedicated to the authors of "Design Patterns: Elements of Reusable Object-Oriented Software" and includes information about the book, the authors, and the design patterns themselves.

www.ingramcontent.com/pod-product-compliance
Lightning Source LLC
Chambersburg PA
CBHW080955220526
45465CB00008BA/3299